HOLLAND

Herman Scholten

2

Copyright:
Bears Publishing,
Postbus 1482,
1300 BL Almere.

Compilation and photography:
Herman Scholten, Almere.

Responsible for other photographs:
Benelux Press: *pages 1, 57(bottom)*
Rondo: *pages 5*
Capital Press: *pages 7 and 124 and cover (1x)*
Aerophoto Schiphol: *pages 8/9, 30/31, 46, 47, 54(2x), 58, 76/77, 93/94, 129, 134, 138, 141*
Beeldbank en Uitgeefprojekten: *pages 26, 31, 53(2x), 69, 87(2x), 90(3x), 103, 110*
Fotostock Amsterdam: *pages 33, 86(2x) 100, 114(2x), 131, 132*
J.L.J. Tersteeg Ridderkerk: *pages 38(2x)*
W. Janszen Harderwijk: *pages 49(1x), 50(3x)*
Bert Blokhuis: *pages 60, 99*
KLM-fotodienst: *pages 6, 7 and 19 (1x)*
Rijksmuseum Paleis Het Loo E. Boeijinga: *pages 82*
Bloemenveiling Aalsmeer: *pages 18, 19*
Meetkundige Dienst Afdeling Grafische Techniek: *Pages 118, 119*

Text: Frederik Wiedijk, Blokzijl

Cover design: Tjasker Design

Lithography: Nederlof Repro Heemstede

Publication and Distribution:
Bears Publishing Almere
Tel: 036 - 530 0003
Fax: 036 - 530 0630

Translation:
Caroline Kimman, Soest

ISBN: 90-5495-904-5

Holland, surprisingly versatile!

All around the world the name 'Holland' is much better known than 'The Netherlands'. The Republic of the Netherlands, which has been a kingdom since 1815, was formed in 1648 following the Peace treaty of Munster. The word 'Holland' has a much older sound to it. It is derived from the word Holtland, which means Houtland (Woodland). Forests and marshes covered the land.

Until about the year 1000 squirrels could jump from treetop to treetop from Antwerp to Groningen and from Maastricht to Alkmaar without ever touching the ground. But the Hol(t)landers burned the wood for cooking and fireplaces. Or used it to build houses or ships or to make clogs. A ban was enforced against cutting down trees on what measly little was left of the forests. Timber could only be imported. Using wood as a fuel was not affordable. Luckily Holland had a good supply of moor-peat and bog-peat. The peat was used for fuel.

Mud-peat had a high calorie value, and was dug from under water and dried on land. Many of the lakes in Holland were created due to the digging for peat. These lakes can be found in the 'old' Holland as well as in the provinces Western-Overijssel and Friesland.

From an aeroplane you can clearly see peat areas that have not been reclaimed and lakes. These have been made into natural areas. Some areas, such as 'De Weerribben' in Northwest Overijssel, 'De grote Peel' and 'De Biesbos', became National Parks. Another phenomenon in Holland is the control over water. Much of the polderland lies up to 6 metres under sea-level. The inland waterways are kept level artificially with the aid of dykes, pumping-stations and system of reservoirs for superfluous polderwater. These are mostly computer generated so that during periods of rain or drought the water level remains the same.

Holland is not only lowland. During the different ice ages banks of specific soil and sand dunes were created. The Utrechtse Heuvelrug, the Veluwe, Drenthe and Twente are considerably higher than the surrounding areas where the river- and marsh delta's are. Even in Limburg and in parts of North-Brabant they do not have to worry about wet feet. That is, if the rivers do not overflow their banks.

The IJssel can be considered as one of the most beautiful rivers with lovely old Hanseatic towns such as Zutphen, Deventer, Zwolle and Kampen. Surrounding the IJsselmeer, which used to be called the 'Zuiderzee' (South Sea) before the Afsluitdijk was built in 1932, you can find magnificent old towns and villages. The outdoor Zuiderzee-museum in Enkhuizen lets you relive the history of fishing and trade.

Of course we do not want to avoid the big cities. 's-Gravenhage (Den Haag) is the town where our government is situated, not in our capital. Amsterdam is the capital of the Netherlands. It is no wonder that we dedicate a number of pages to it in this edition. Rotterdam is still the largest trade and trans-shipping harbour in the world.

Utrecht, situated in the centre of the country is sometimes called 'Bishops town'. Until the reformation, around 1568 (Statue breaking period), the Bishops of Utrecht reigned over a large part of the northern provinces. In Utrecht you can still find traces rich Roman life. Maastricht, the oldest city in the Netherlands and 's Hertogenbosch, capital of the provence North-Brabant, are where 'Burgundians' (the more flamboyant population) live. As in many place south of the main rivers, carnival is celebrated with exuberance. Eindhoven is the largest city in the south. Its size is mainly due to the Philips company.

The islands in Zeeland are also special with their pretty towns and villages. Vlissingen lies proudly at the mouth of the Schelde. A visit to the Delta Works is recommended as the Dutch knowledge of water control can be observed, such as the closing of the two slides across the Nieuwe Waterweg.

We will also look at the northern provinces Friesland and Groningen. Friesland and the adjoining area of lakes in Northwest Overijssel is a paradise for lovers of watersports. A large rental fleet of sailing ships such as Aken, Tjalken and Klippers or even modern yachts and motorboats is at your disposal.

The Wadden islands are a very popular holiday destination. Netherlands has the image of 'The Land of windmills, tulips, national costumes and clogs'. Luckily there is much more to be discovered as this book will show. Windmills do often dominate the countryside. For example, at Kinderdijk where nineteen windmills on a row keep the polder dry. A selection of 'industrial' windmills can be found at the Zaanse Schans. These include wood sawing mills, paint- and oil windmills, mustard and peeling mills.

The most famous regional costume is worn in Staphorst, just north of Zwolle. The costumes in Marken and Volendam are more for tourists. In Bunschoten, Spakenburg, Urk and Zeeland you can still find people wearing the costume as their daily dress. The younger generation does not consider it fit to wear to a disco though.

The bulb-fields are situated in a line behind the dunes from Den Haag till Den Helder. The most well known places are Lisse and Hillegom (home to the Keukenhof), Limmen and Breezand. This is where the 'Tulips from Amsterdam' come from. In the IJsselmeer polders more and more bulb-fields can be seen. A surplus of cows(milk) and pigs made the farmers search for alternative sources of income. Many now run eel and sheath-fish hatchery or have redeveloped regional products that are grown eco- and biologically friendly.

The Dutch farmer is used to adapting to the need of the soil. The people of the Netherlands are proud and hospitable. They cherish their countryside and monumental heritage, and are fully supported by the government.

You can not lump all Dutch people together. People living in the west are usually pretty open. The people in Friesland and Groningen will only open up after they get to know you. The population in the south really know how to enjoy a party.

It is remarkable that English and other languages are spoken by most people in the Netherlands. An ex-minister once said: 'It is because we have so many foreign neighbours'.

4

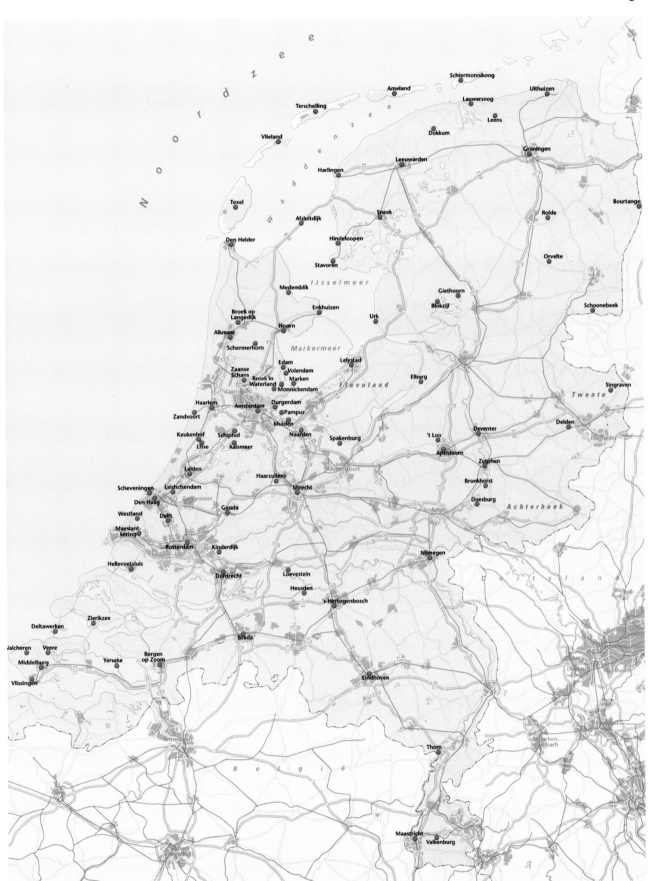

Terminal

Air Traffic Control Tower

Departure Hall

Schiphol Airport, 'Amsterdam Airport', is ideally located near to the capital. Train and road connections to other large cities such as Utrecht, The Hague and Rotterdam are easy. Travelling to the rest of Holland using domestic flights is easy.

People from other continents often choose to arrive at Schiphol Airport before travelling to other parts of Europe. Schiphol is home to the KLM-fleet, the first airline in the world and has more than 75 years of experience.

When observing the busy activity at Schiphol, it is difficult to imagine that long ago the waves on the Haarlemmermeer (lake) ruled. This lake was milled dry by many windmills and the pump-engine Cruquius (now a museum). 'Amsterdam Airport' now lies (safely) some 4 metres under North Sea-level.

In the vicinity of the airport you find many international offices and distributors.

8   Amsterdam

'Large Mokum', this is the name given to the city of Amsterdam by jiddish salesmen in the time of the painter Rembrandt van Rijn.

True, Amsterdam is a 'Large City'. It is a very special city, as can be seen from the air. Many Dutch towns have been designed using rectangular and square shapes to build up the town. But Amsterdam was built in a circular shape using a canal-network.

'Amstelredam', in latin 'Amsteloda-mum' was situated at the mouth of the river Amstel from around 1270. At that point the Amstel flowed into the River IJ. It started as a dam with locks which had to protect the Amstelland from the nearing Zuiderzee and the water from the IJ. Around 1300 Amsterdam obtained city-rights. A toll was charges for the import of Hamburg beer into Holland. Still a remarkable shipping route was established between Hamburg and Amsterdam. At a later time this was extended with trade between the Oostzee (east sea, north of Holland) area and Vlaanderen in Belgium.

The Eastern Sea towns traded grain. This is why the port of Amsterdam became a grain storage place for Northern Netherlands and was the largest trading city of Holland. The lively city of Amsterdam is great cosmopolitan town with almost 24-hour night-life.

Amsterdam is very pedestrian-friendly. Safely park your car in a parking area or take public transport into Mokum. In the city centre, within the canal-network, practically everything is within walking distance. En route there is lots to see and enjoy. This is what the next pages are about.

Canal-network

Centraal Station

Noord-Zuidhollands koffiehuis

There are many shipping companies that run water-bus trips on the canals of Amsterdam. They are situated near Central Station. Good tour-guides inform the passengers of the many unique buildings, bridges and monuments along the docks canals. These tours can be heard in practically any language.

Water-busses are comfortable but low. This is to allow the boat to travel under the many fixed bridges. From these bridges it is exciting to watch the boats manoeuvre through tight spots. But a collision is always prevented.

Damrak

Many shopping streets and squares are exclusively for pedestrians.

Weather permitting, there are many terraces on which you can sit and enjoy a drink. In 1655 the building of the Royal Palace on the Dam was concluded. It was originally built as a Town Hall. Opposite the Palace is the National Monument, a monument for those who died in the 1940-1945 war.

Damrak

Monument on the Dam

Royal Palace on the Dam

New Metropolis

A replica of the Verenigd Oostindische Compagnie (United East Indies Company) ship 'Amsterdam' is moored in front of the Maritime Museum.

Shipyards and warehouses owned by the V.O.C. merchants are located nearby, on the island of Oostenburg.

Montelbaan tower

Maritime Museum and V.O.C. ship 'Amsterdam'

A great deal of these warehouses can still be seen today as they have been converted into luxury apartments. The exterior has been preserved.

Water is very important to the city of Amsterdam. The canals made delivery to the warehouses possible. Goods from all over the world were stored here before distribution to other harbours or to the hinter land. There are a great number of houseboats and pleasure yachts in the canals of Amsterdam. The canal water is kept clean because of nightly flushing.

Zuiderkerk

Stopera

For nearly three quarters of a century the council of Amsterdam have thought about and discussed building a new Town Hall. At the same time there emerged a need for a new large opera house.

It was the architect Holzbauer who finally was able to combine the two projects. The result is the 'Stopera': a Town hall and a music theatre in one, built on 3075 piles.

The exterior gave reason for much debate amongst the inhabitants of Amsterdam, but the building that opened in September 1986 worked so well that now everyone is proud of their new addition.

Amstel

Skinny bridge

Theater Carré

Holland Casino

Wester Church

The Zuider Church competes with the Large Church of Blokzijl for the title of 'Oldest Protestant Church in the Netherlands'. At Whit in 1611 the first reformed protestant service was held in the Amsterdam Church. This kind of service had been held in Blokzijl in 1609. But this House of God was just a simple church hall. In the following years building in Blokzijl continued. The Church and Tower of Blokzijl with the shape of a Greek Cross was completed in 1662. The graceful Zuider Church Tower was built in 1614 and considered to the prettiest in Amsterdam.

Herengracht

The Leidseplein (square) is probably the largest terrace in Amsterdam, although the one on Rembrandsplein is pretty large too.

  Actually on warm summer days terraces all over Amsterdam are full of people from all over the world enjoying a drink and soaking up the atmosphere.

Leidse plein

Bartolotti house on the Herengracht

Where in the world does one find so many different gables such as in the hart of Amsterdam. During the Dutch Golden Age (1600 - 1700) the Amsterdam merchants tried to outdo each other in splendour with their canal houses. Many different types of gables can be seen, such as the Step-, Bell-, Neck-, Spout- and Cornice gable.

On the many different gables and house marks, each one has a history of its own.

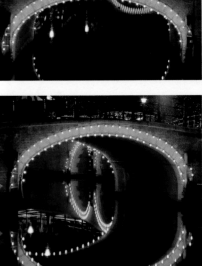

Herengracht

Reguliersgracht

Skinny Bridge

Damrak

Amsterdam is considered most beautiful on a sweet summer evening just after dusk with the traffic a little quieter. The ten-thousands of lights define the contours of the many bridges and reflect in the canal water. Many of the old monuments and futuristic buildings are floodlit.

Rijksmuseum

The 'Red Light District' has its own charms. Real Amsterdammers, mostly seagoing people and tradesmen, do not seem to have any problem with the district.

Montelbaan Tower

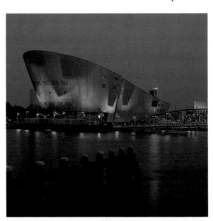

New Metropolis

Maritime museum

'ArenA'

Aalsmeer is situated near Schiphol Airport. Since around 1850, many kinds of flowers and plants are cultivated here. Naturally the world's largest flower auction is located in Aalsmeer.

The auction is held in very modern complex using the latest advanced logistics to ensure quick sales and purchases. Nearly 3000 growers are a member of this cooperative company. A testing laboratory for flower cultivation and a horticultural college are also located in Aalsmeer.

Auction Hall

The flowers are exported to all over the world. An auctioned bouquet of flowers can often be on sale in Tokyo or New York the very same day.

At the National Flower Trade Exhibition is held annually in Aalsmeer. Growers and merchants from all over the world come to learn about new varieties and innovative horticultural technology.

Export by air

20   Zandvoort

Many people, especially the people from Amsterdam, come to Zandvoort for relaxation and recreation. The railway train has its last stop nearly on the beach. There is an excellent bicycle network right through the dunes.

There are many terraces to sit and enjoy a drink or some food. Zandvoort has a nice village centre and there are many organized events to entertain you. If it is a bit of excitement you are looking for then the casino or the race-track are the places to be.

Boulevard

Gravenstenen Bridge

Amsterdam Gate

The painter Frans Hals and the 'inventor' of letterpress printing, Laurens Janszoon Coster are Haarlem's most famous inhabitants. A statue of Coster stands on the Grote Markt (Large Market) in this town. Haarlem is the capital of the provence North-Holland. There is museum is dedicated to Frans Hals and his contemporaries. Displayed around the Grote Markt are a large number of monuments, Haarlem has more than a thousand monuments.

Teylers Hofje (Courtyard)

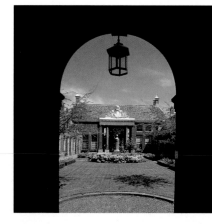

Town hall

Laurens Jansz. Coster

St. Bavo

One of the many monuments is the Saint Bavo, a Gothic Basilica shaped like a cross, which was erected in several phases between 1400 and 1520. There is a second Saint Bavo in Haarlem, the 'Cathedral Basilica' (1895 - 1930). Here you will find the magnificent Adema-organ, built between 1921 and 1923. Regularly concerts are held on this organ.

The banks of the river Spaarne in and outsid the city are diverse and lovely to look at. Lovers of antiques will enjoy Haarlem very much, there is a lot on offer. There are many beautifully restored 'hofjes' (courtyards) well worth a visit. An afternoon can be filled by looking at and trying to decipher the texts on the many gables and signs. These tell the tale of the ancient old trades and crafts.

The Weigh House

Mustard Mill 'De Huisman'

Paint Mill 'De Kat'

Trade on the banks of the River Zaan was mostly dependent on the wind. The windmills worked several old crafts. In 1622 mill called 'De Ooievaar' (The Stork) started as an oil mill. 'De Huisman' (The House man) still produces the very well known coarse Zaans mustard since 1780.

'De Zoeker' (The Searcher) is over 50 years younger and the paint mill 'De Kat' (The Cat) dates back to 1781.

    The youngest of the five mills is 'De Gekroonde Poelenberg' where timber has been sawn since 1869. In a hexagonal bulwark the protestants (opponents of Philip II) resisted a raid and a seige of the Spanish army.

    The memory is kept alive in the picturesque Zaan neighbourhood reconstructed with examples of traditional timbered buildings.

Kalverringdijk

't Koopmanshuys

What 'Albert Heijn of 1887' looked like then can be seen in the Grocery Museum. The museum shop shows how the now large supermarket chain started with products such as petroleum lamps, bag carriers, scales on chains and many other items sold back then.

The open air museum exhibits a large number of wooden houses transported to the museum in one piece. Some of the houses have been compiled. Part of the restaurant 'De Walvisch' (The Whale) is made from an old orphanage in Westzaan. The top floor comes from an 18th century herring-net house in Koog aan de Zaan.

During the French period the 'Dutch Waterline' developed to keep the advancing French troops at bay. This Waterline was extended with 'The Stelling of Amsterdam' in the 19th and 20th century.

The Stelling was shaped in a circle with an outline of 135 kilometres and consisted of 42 fortresses all round the capital. The idea was that the troops could pull back to within this area if the outer line of defence did not hold. During a seige the population would not starve as there was enough space for agriculture. Heavy artillery was placed in between the fortresses and if necessary the land outside the circle could be flooded.

Fortunately the Stelling has never needed to be used, in fact it was out-of-date by the time it was built. In 1996, the Stelling of Amsterdam has been placed on the World Heritage List of the Unesco as a historic monument. Some of the fortress guard-houses are still occupied, the one at Fort Durgerdam for instance. Most of the stellings are open to the public. The fortresses are a part of the landscape and sometimes even blend in with its surroundings.

There is a 135 kilometre bicycle route along all fortresses.

A typical Dutch expression is 'Voor Pampus liggen', literally meaning 'Being drunk'.
The phrase is derived from the time that the ships of the V.O.C. (United East Indian Company) could not reach Amsterdam easily because of the shallow waters of the Zuiderzee. This shallow part of the sea was called Pampus.

The ships had to wait until the 'Ship Camels', a special kind of dock, would carry them across the sandbank. During the long wait the shipowner arranged for women, drink and fresh food to be brought on board.
Later a fortress was build on this sandbank as part of the 'Dutch Waterline' which protected the Amsterdam 'Orange' locks.

For a while it was used as a storage area for the government, but now the island is open for exploration of the any secret passages and vaults. The view from the fortress over the IJsselmeer is fantastic.

28   Broek in Waterland

The houses in Broek in Waterland are mainly made from timber. The reason is fear of flooding. The houses were built on top of stone foundations that served as a barricade.

The entrance to the house could be reached by a wooden or stone staircase.

Standing on the edge of the pulpit inthe sixteenth century Late Gothic Church is an hour-glass. This was to prevent the minister of speaking longer than one hour.

Mostly commuters live in the many different kinds of houses in Broek in Waterland. A typical thing about the houses in Broek in Waterland is that many of the gables are not lined up.

Skating fun

Winter in Broek in Waterland

The Weigh House and Bell Tower

The pattern of the streets and the typical Dutch canal-system in Monnickendam has barely changed since 1650. On both sides of the harbour one of the oldest trades in Monnickendam can be seen: ship-building and repairs.

The Waag, a weigh house, is located near this harbour. The location is most charming as is the whole of the 'living open air museum'. And there is no fee.

In the second half of the 17th century the Waag was decorated with lovely pilaster gables. Next to the Waag is the Bell Tower.

It is striking monument of which is unknown when and why it was built. The building was made with bricks and the top was made with timber. The tower owes it's name to the carillon which is housed inside. It is now the only complete carillon of that period in the Netherlands.

The bells chime every hour and half hour. The Bell Tower is a captivating sight on the skyline of Monnickendam, especially when viewed from the Gouw Sea. During a severe winter a very typical Dutch sport takes place on the Gouw Sea: ice sailing.

Ice sailing on the Gouw Sea

After the monks left the island in the fourteenth century, the dykes were neglected. The agriculture and cattle farming made way for fishing. In times when the Marken population fished for whales, the island became more prosperous due to the try-houses (whale-oil manufacturers).

At the end of the 19th century there were 163 fishing boats, but when the Zuiderzee was dammed in the people of Marken had to find an alternative source of income. The solution was found in using the boats for the transport of hay.

The hay that came from Marken had the reputation of being the best possible for your cattle!
When the winds reached gale force 10 and Northwest storm forced the North Sea water via the
Waddenzee into the Zuiderzee the islanders were warned by a rattle. People had to prepare for
yet another flooding.

 The lighthouse on Marken is called 'het Witte Paard' (the White Horse). The light was
generated by gas and the foghorn used compressed air. During long and severe winters, drift-
ice would reach up to the lighthouse or even in through the windows.

'Burly'. This is the best possible description for the male traditional costume from Volendam. The costumes for the women are considered charming and elegant. The traditional costumes of the 'Dutch cheese girls' as worn at international exhibitions is a variation of the Volendam costume.

When the Zuiderzee was 'open', the Volendammers fished using wooden ships: Botters and Kwakken. Presently the odd fisherman owns steel ships that isspecialized in fishing for eel and pike-perch.

They are not the only ones fishing. Their main competitor are Cormorants. Cormorants are protected birds, but with a daily requirement of as much fish as their own weight.

Together with Edam Volendam forms a joint municipality.
Volendam is more than just a tourist centre and a fishing village.

In the north of Volendam there is a large commercial area with many different industries. Volendam with its maze of fishermen's houses built on poles and a unique open harbour is still in original state. The timbered little church built on stone dates back to 1658.

Fish-market ☖

Kwakel Bridge

'Boerenverdriet' (Farmers Sorrow) is a name of the ditch that meanders through Edam. A dam in the river Ye created this ditch at the beginning of the 12th century. In 1357, the rapidly growing Edam was granted city-rights including the right to hold annual fetes and to have a toll-free harbour.

The Kwakelbrug is probably the most photographed classic drawbridge.

The old town centre and especially the Kwakelsteeg still has lovely characteristic Waterland houses in the Kwakelsteeg partially made from wood.

There is still a working shipyard for repairs or maintenance to traditional botters and kwakken (fishingboats).

There is a very nice view indeed from the Schepenmakersdijk of the lovely tea pavilions and tea domes on the water. The Bell Tower of Edam with its cheerful carillon was built in the 15th century.

The tower nearly collapsed in 1972, but it was fortunately prevented in time. Other object of interest are the late-gothic Large Church with its beautiful leaded windows, the museum set in the old stone built house in Edam (approx. 1540) including a floating cellar and of course the Lutheran Church from 1740.

'Boerenverdriet'

Shipyard

Cheese Market

Edam Cheese has become a brand name. It is not only produced in Edam but throughout the Netherlands and even abroad. Cheese markets are still held in the summer months. They are not held for trade purposes, but for their tourist value.

Edam cheeses called 40+ weigh between 1,7 and 2 kilograms. They look almost globular, are firm and slice well. Connoisseurs describe the taste as 'savoury and refreshing'. The Proveniers-hofje, where many a generation enjoyed a quiet autumn of life, dates from 1555.

Proveniershofje

Cheese Market

Alkmaar has a long history of providing trade, schooling, infrastructure and care for the surrounding region. The world famous large Cheese Market is held in front of the Waag, every Friday from April to October.
Before being rebuilt as a Weigh House in 1582, the building was the H. Geesthuis Chapel.
The unique bells and horseman play in the tower of the Weigh House is well worth watching closely.
Over the years a number of canals have been filled in, but there are still enough canals left for a trip around the town in a canalboat.

Kuipers Bridge

Wildemanshofje

Cruising along the water you have a great view of several characteristic 'hofjes', courtyards, such as the Splinter and the Wildemanshofje as seen above and many beautiful large merchants houses. In years gone by toll was collected here from the incoming freight ships. Presently it is an office of the harbour master.

The rear sides of the houses along the Achterdam and Fnidsen are well suited for unloading freight from boats. On the corner of the Verdronkenoord and the Bierkade you will find the Accijns Tower. The 'Large' or 'Sint Laurens' Church is a unique example of Brabant gothic architecture in Holland. It holds a very beautiful looking organ which plays beautifully too.

Accijns House

Stompe Tower E

Stompe Tower D

First windmill of the set

The excess water in the Schermer Polder (lowland) needs to be transported up four metres. It takes three windmills to do this by milling the water upwards in several stages. The middle windmill is situated on the Noordervaart 2 and is a working mill and a museum. On the ground floor you can see the original 19th century millers cottage. Many authentic utilities are on view.

Glass plates have been installed in the floors to give an insight into the working of this type of windmill. The attics, which can be climbed all the way to the top of the mill, show many different millers tools.

Going through an auction house on a barge. This is possible in Broek op Langedijk. At regular times in the summer it is possible to participate in the oldest navigated vegetable auction. This is only done to uphold the tradition. The Broeker Auction is more an inside and outside museum with a unique collection of barges, which in earlier times carried many different kinds of cabbages and other vegetables. The museum is very proud of its historic collection of horticultural tools and West Friesian traditional dress. There is an animal farm and boat trips, but these are additional attractions.

40   Hoorn

At the beginning of the 14th century Hoorn started out as a settlement for merchants from Denmark and North Germany. It was located where the river Gouw meets the Zuiderzee.

In 1356, Hoorn was granted town rights and by then already had a Weigh House. Between 1500 and 1600 the city proved to be the most important harbour for export and import on the Zuiderzee.

A statue of Jan Pieterz. Coen (1587-1629) is located in front of the Weigh House. This famous son of Hoorn was a natural strategist and merchant who laid the foundations for the Dutch rule over the Indonesian Archipelago. He would have like to named the city of Batavia (now Djakarta) Nieuw-Hoorn.

From the remarkable semi-round Hoofd Tower located at the inner harbour you can see the 'Brown Sailing Fleet' which partly use Hoorn as its permanent port. The three ship's boys of the 'Bonte Koe' have been immortalized in bronze on the quayside. Nearly every Dutch boy knows the adventures of Padde, Rolf and Hajo who sailed on the Bonte Koe. Johan Fabricius wrote the book.

Oosterpoort

The West Friesian Museum is well known for active acquisition, especially concerning the history of Hoorn and the United East Indies Company. The museum proudly presents 25 chambers and rooms showing treasures from our rich past. Expositions of certain relevant subjects are also held at the museum.
The fine-looking monument was the seat of the States Council (1632).

West Friesian Museum

From whatever side you look at the Oosterpoort, with its Italian Renaissance style, it boasts a wealthy old ambience next to the typically Dutch Neck, Bell and Step gables.

There are three Bossu-houses and each depict a battle fought on the Zuiderzee in 1573 when Holland was engaged in the Eighty-Years-of-War with Spain.

Dromedaris

The Saint Pancreas Church and the 'Dromedaris' are the two most obvious buildings in the old part of Enkhuizen. The Dromedaris was built in 1540 as part of the fortifications and in 1649 two floors were added.

Twenty-five years after the Dromedaris was built the Hemony brothers received an order to cast a carillon of 24 bells for the little dome tower. Their music still rings out over the harbours. Villains were once imprisoned in the tower rooms. Fishermen used to unload their abundant catches at the foot of the Dromedaris. Now expositions and other cultural activities are held there.

Spui

Zuiderzee Museum with Company Bridge

During the first half of the Eighty-Years-of-War the town of Enkhuizen was at its peak of economic growth due to the favourable location on the Zuiderzee and the enterprising drive of local merchants. Enkhuizen was an 'Orange' town and due to the strategic location it became the home harbour for the fighting protestant Fleet. They controlled the Zuiderzee. When Enkhuizen became one of the six locations of the East India Company the town expanded with houses and storage buildings.

Harbour

The outdoor museum, located just behind the old part of Enkhuizen, consists of a selection of cottages, places of work and shops. It gives a picture of the little Zuiderzee town in times gone by.

You will see a barrel maker, tannery, steam wash house, cheese storage house and many fisherman's cottages. These give an insight into not only the glory days of the Golden Age, but especially the sober living conditions of the hard working population.

Koepoort

Enkhuizen flourished only for a short period. In 1650 it had 30.000 inhabitants, eighty years later 1200 and a century later 5000. Almost 1600 houses were torn down in about one hundred years.

Outdoor Museum

44   Medemblik

Bonifacius Church

In 1289 town privileges were granted to Medemblik by Count Floris V. It was then the first town of West-Friesland. There are many places of interest, but Radboud Castle is Medemblik's pride and joy.

Originally the stronghold was built as a square fortress with round and square towers. During the following centuries it started to deteriorate until in 1890 the architect Cuypers rebuilt one of the round corner towers. The moats were dug out again in 1936.

Next to the Town Hall you will find the station where the famous steam train runs between Hoorn and Medemblik. Alternatively five steam trains pull the historic carriages.

Radboud Castle

Steam train Hoorn - Medemblik

The Steam Machine Museum is located in a beautiful industrial monument. It used to be a steam grinder 'De Vier Noorderkoggen'.

Steam Grinder

Originally the present navy town of Den Helder was a fishing village on the island Huisduinen and developed from 1500.
In 1774 the village was moved to a location along the Marsdiep on the Helderse Zeewering.

In 1811 emperor Napoleon visited Huisduinen and realised that this would make a perfect position for a stronghold. The fortress Kijkduin is large enough to house up to 700 soldiers.

Fort Kijkduin

Between 1825 and 1876 the harbour town of 'Nieuwendiep' (as it now was being called) flourished due to the digging of the Great North Holland Canal. Unfortunately this did not last for very long as another important canal, the North Sea Canal between IJmuiden and Amsterdam was being dug.

At present the economy of, now called, Den Helder is dependent upon tourism and the fact that the Royal Navy has its fleet stationed here. There are very many activities in Den Helder connected with navigation.

Light House 'Huisduinen'

It was on 28th May 1932 that in the presence of Queen Wilhelmina the final gap was closed between the Zuiderzee and the Wadden Sea / North Sea. The south side of the Afsluitdijk was named the IJsselmeer. Finally the provence North-Holland was connected to the provence Friesland.
Many of the often weak dykes around the lake were less of a risk during storms, like the great storm of 1916. Sea water became sweet water.

Drainage was improving for all the areas surrounding the IJsselmeer, due to control over the level of the water. The man behind the Zuiderzee project was the engineer Cornelis Lely. He delivered his proposal for the project in 1891, but died in 1929 so did not live to see the completion of the Afsluitdijk. Already in 1667 Hendrik Stevin, son of Simon, proposed to close the gaps between the Wadden Islands and the main land. His plan was not taken seriously and technology was not advanced enough then. Eight proposals in total were sent to the government on the subject.

Before closing the Dijk, the polder named the Wieringermeer needed to become dry land. It would take until 1934 before this polder would be ready for cultivation. In 1945, during German occupation, this polder again was flooded. Now the Noord-Oostpolder (48.0000 ha) and Flevoland (97.000 ha) have been cultivated. There has been the intention to create the Markerwaard, the final polder, situated just south of the Afsluitdijk. But strong objections from environmental organisations (forage for birds), watersport lovers and many individuals has erupted against creating land where there is now water. The monument on the Afsluitdijk (Watch Tower) carries the text: 'A people that live, build for their future'.

The Wadden Sea is located between the mainland of Holland and the Northwest of Germany and surrounded by a row of Dutch islands.

The water in this sea is fairly shallow and one must contend with the tide and the beacons. On hot summer days the 'Brown Fleet' sail around. These used to be ships for freight and fishing, but now mainly used for recreational trips lasting one to several days. The Wadden Islands Texel, Vlieland, Terschelling and Schiermonnikoog are popular tourist destinations.

Very fast and luxurious ferries sail alongside tjalken, klippers, aken and other flat bottomed boats. At low tide several sandbanks become dry.

These become ideal sunning beaches for the seals. After some years of problems with the seals, the population is well again.

Containing the pollution level has made the Wadden Sea rich in food for the seals and the thousands of birds. The Wadden sea is a very popular stop-over for birds before and after the migration.

The sea can be rough too at times. The waves are then short and fierce. Luckily there is a very well organised rescue operation in the whole area. Inspection following a severe storm will often show that sandbanks and parts of an island have 'walked' so that the channel has been moved by Mother Nature.

'Het Noorden' windmill

Texel is our oldest island and is also called the Pearl of the Wadden Islands. It has unspoilt dunes, a rich foliage, thousands of birds and a flowing landscape.

Old Schild Harbour

There is a monument in Oosterend for the transcendant Texel Sheep. Sheep are very prominent on the island. The ground and dry climate in the spring are ideal for farming sheep. The animals are not very demanding.

Texel farmers keep the Texels Pedigree Sheep to maintain the breed. It used to be that sheep were mainly kept for their milk or wool. The Texel Pedigree Sheep is as good as the English Sheep.

Jutter Museum

Blind alley

East-Vlieland is the only village on the 21 kilometre long island. The west of the island is a large sandbank. It used to be a gathering point for ships on their way to the East Sea or the Atlantic Ocean.

In the 17th century Vlieland accommodated 70 'commodores', captains of whaling boats or of merchants ships.

Village Street

With a height of 40 metres the highest dune of the Wadden Islands, the Vuurboets Dune, is a likely place for a Light House. The Light House gives ships a chance to orientate.

Until 1836 the light consisted of a large fire. The coals for the fire were kept in a barn, called a Boet. Since 1909 the current 18 metre high Light House has taken over that task.

Light House

52   Terschelling (Skylge)

Buoy Depot

The island Terschelling, also named Skylge, is located between the islands Vlieland and Ameland. It is around 15 to 20 kilometres north west off the Friesian mainland coast.

In the Commandeurs Street you can find the Behouden Huys Museum. The museum contains several rooms in the style of the previous century. The bond between the island and the sea can be seen in the pilotage and rescue and life-saving service on view here.

Commodore Houses

'Brandaris'

The Light House 'Brandaris' was named after the Irish Abbot St. Brandaan who according to legend made marvellous sea trips.
The Brandaris accommodates the coastguard centre for the whole Wadden Island area. Every ship movements on the Wadden Sea are checked here, day and night.

The island Ameland can count on more than 1 million nights spent by tourists, each year. The population used to survive on intensive whaling. You can see this still on the gables of the commodores houses, for instance in Nes and Hollum. Whale ribs are sometimes used to stake out property.

From time to time sperm-whale wash up onto the shores. If the wreckers are lucky they can find precious amber inside the whale. It is worth a lot of money.

When visiting the island, the impressive Light House and the modern Nature Centre Ameland are both well worth a visit. At low tide it is possible to walk from Friesland to Ameland, the so-called 'Wad Walking'.

Light House

Commodore House

The Wad

Behind the impressive locks of Lauwersoog lies the complex consisting of a harbour for pleasure yachts, a fishing harbour with storage and the Schiermonnikoog ferry service. It is the smallest of the Wadden Islands.

The name of the only village is the same as the island and refers to the lay brothers who made the dykes there in the 15th century. The word Schier means grey, the colour of the monk's habit and the word Oog means island.

Light House   *Lauwersoog Harbour*

'Zeldenrust' Windmill

Four centuries ago the town of Dokkum became enclosed by a rampart, a fortification. Still the six bastions surround the beautiful centre of the town. The town is located on a crossing of land and water ways. The missionary Bonifatius (754) was murdered here and so Dokkum became a place of pilgrimage. The peeling mills situated at the southern bastions date back to 1849 and 1862.

The Oldehove (1532) is the tower that looks like a stump and is right in the centre of Leeuwarden. It used to be part of a five-aisled church, but because the foundations were too light the tower was never completed. The church itself was demolished in 1595.

Of the remaining monuments in Leeuwarden the Weigh House is most dominating. You can see a large number of brick-work arched bridges dating back to the 16th and 17th century.

The Weigh House

'Oldehove'

The province Friesland is renowned for its Eleven City Race, skating on natural ice. Eleven cities is all the province has. There are many picturesque villages. The inhabitants of Friesland are friendly but determined people that cling to their own identity and language. Friesian is an official language. The language is hardly understandable for non-friesians which sometimes leads to communication problems when 'importing' from other parts of Holland.

Luckily the hospitable Friesians are prepared to speak to 'foreigners' is the Dutch language. The south-western part of the provence is the most abounding in water of all of the Netherlands. As soon as winter proves to be its most severe, the Friesians put on their skates and inspect the eleven cities. Many thousands of skaters from all over the country travel up to join them.

In summer you can cycle or surf along the race route. There is also a tradition called 'skûtje silen'. This is a Sailing Match between Friesian Spritsail barges. These used to be used for cargo. These barges transported cow dung to the bulb fields, potatoes to the towns along the Zuiderzee and returned with freights for home. A typical aspect of the tjalkes and other flat bottomed boats are that they have lee-boards. Much of Friesland water is too shallow for ships with a keel. By lowering the board on leeside the boat would not drift.

Also typical of Friesland are the black-patched cows. With a dreamy look in their eyes they turn grass into milk. Many city children do not realise that milk is made by cows and not at the factory or supermarket!

The white square Light House and the industrial harbour of Harlingen confirm that this harbour wishes to continue to play a part in the Dutch sea trade. Harlingen has been involved in fishing for centuries. Since half way the eighties the robust fishing cutter from Urk dominate the fishing fleet. The fish auction of Harlingen has a turn-over which puts in the top five of the country. Luckily most of all the old gables and monuments are still intact.

'Havenmantsje'

Light House

Town hall

Waterpoort

Sneek is the centre of the thriving world of watersports in Friesland. It is surrounded by large and small lakes.

Every year, at the beginning of August, the Sneekweek is held with many activities. The highlight is of course the sailing regatta. This event together with the large fair, draws all Friesians from all over the country to the town.

The covered harbour is one of the largest in the area. Once the city was completely enclosed by walls and two land gates and the still remaining Sneek Water Gate. This monument is a covered bridge which was built in 1613. It was completely restored in 1878 and in the only one of its kind in Holland. Sneek has a very nice shopping centre and you can enjoy going out too.

The town hall, which originates in the 15th century, now looks as it was rebuilt in the 18th century. The gable has been sculptured in the Friesian Rococo style.

Town Hall

Lock-keeper's house

Near the lock-keeper's house with the smart small bell tower, built in 1619, you will find the covered 'Lie bench'. On it there are always some old Hindeloopen skippers who can tell a tale or two about their fishing days. Above this bench a mural has been painted depicting 'a miraculous catch'.

The traditional costume of Hindeloopen is very typical for the town. Hindeloopen painting can interestingly enough be found on many different kind of objects, but specifically on furniture. Even some forms of transport have been painted in the style.

Spike Sleigh

In fact the Mistress of Stavoren was not a very nice person. She requested her captain to bring her something valuable back from the East Sea area. When he brought back golden corn she explodes in anger and commanded the corn to be dumped in the Zuidersea. At present on that spot lies the 'Vrouwen' sandbank on which wild corn grows. The sandbank made it difficult to reach the once so prosperous harbour of Stavoren.

Stavoren flourished especially in the eleventh century and later again in the 16th century. Now with the waterway to the yacht harbour restored Stavoren is a very popular home port for many holiday makers and watersport lovers.

Harbour   *The Mistress of Stavoren*

Gold Office

Groningen can be called the 'Metropolis of the North' and was built on a slope of the 'Hondsrug' around the second century. The Groningen Museum has a collection of earthenware from that period on show.

In the 14th century the rural Groningen became more urban as the population were able to afford to build houses made out of stone.

Martini Tower

Prinsenhof

Groningen Museum

To taste the atmosphere of the old Groningen you must go to the spacious Martini Churchyard. This area is dominated by three buildings, the Martini Church, The County-Hall and the old Saint Maarten school (predecessor of the University of Groningen).

The very nice-looking Prinsenhof has had many functions. Prefects of 'The Brotherhood of Community Lives' lived there. Then the first Bishop of Groningen presided in the Prinsenhof and after 1594 the Stadtholder of Town and Countryside made his living quarters in the building. The University of Groningen was founded in 1614 and called 'The School of Academics'. After Leiden it is the oldest university in the Netherlands, but does boast the oldest students' corps: 'Vindicat at que Polit'.

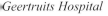
Geertruits Hospital

As the wealth in Groningen grew, the town was able to afford to start building the Martini Tower. The first two parts were ready between 1469 and 1482. The top part including the spire was finalized between 1545 and 1554. The enormous building is named after Saint Martinus van Tours, patron to Groningen. It was built using Bentheimer stone and brick and is lovingly called 'the Old Grey Man'.
The gothic tower has resisted many lightning flashes, a fire and enemy attack. The top part of the tower has been made in the renaissance style with a picture of the horse of Saint Maarten.

Groningen Academy

Small teahouse

There used to be over a hundred Groningen Borgs (Castles), but unfortunately there are only a handful left. Young noblemen lived in these Borgs as they were the lord over the villages. Borg Vrouw Hilda's Heem in Verhilversum is a small castle which was built in the 14th century and renovated at a later date. Here you can see the permanent exhibition ' The history of the Wad and the Land'.

The Borg

This Borg is one the most beautiful of its kind with much of its original furniture. Three
of its wing have top and step gables with corner towers overlooking a large courtyard.
The building is surrounded by a large estate with small buildings, orchards and canals.
Now the Borg is the home of the Groningen Museum for town and countryside.

The Bourtange fortification lies South East of Groningen, near the German border. It played an important role in the Eighty-Years-of-War (1568 - 1648) against Spanish rule.

It was designed by general Diederick of Sonoy. He is also responsible for improving the fortresses of Alkmaar and Blokzijl. Bourtange is located along the primitive but only road in a large, almost uninhabited, swamp area. This road was a trade route in a territory stretching from Coevorden to the Dollar area by the North Sea.

In 1672 the fortification again played an important role in the battle against Christopher Bernhart Freiherr von Galen. Many an army preacher stood in the pulpit in the Garrison Church.

Provisions within the walls of the fortress, such as a mill, farms, storage space, leads us to believe that the people were prepared for a long besiegement. In about 1740 the bastion was very run down and needed much repair and improvement. By then it was not part of any war effort any more.

In 1851 Bourtange was officially taken off the list of military fortresses. Between 1971 and 1982 the buildings have been repaired and renovated and the roads have been improved. As you can see on the photographs the Bourtange fortification has been brought back to its former glory.

Time seems to have stood still in the Drenthe ash-village of Orvelte. Saxon farms with thatched roofs, cobbled roads and ash-trees have either been restored or preserved. The reconstruction is based upon the year 1830.

When walking past the toll houses and entering the beautiful village there is much to look at. Naturally cars are not allowed in the village.

Bruntingerhof is a fine example of farming and many other crafts such as a clog maker's shop, pottery baker and pewterer's workshop can be seen there.

Special events such as harvest, popular local games, sheep sheering are held in summer. They give an impression of life in a small ash-village in those times.

Orvelte has two sheep-pens and every day flocks of about 250 Schoonebeek sheep graze on the heath nearby.

Of course the village centre is very interesting, but the area surrounding Orvelte with its ash-woods, brooks, valleys and waste land are very much worth visiting.

The Hunnebedden (prehistoric sepulchral mounds) on the Drenthe Hondsrug are only remainders of the stone graves which were used many thousands of years ago. Originally a grave entailed a long shaped sand hill with small and large stones to stand as a entrance to the grave.

The grave mounds in fact looked very similar to those used in a later age.

From 2300 B.C. in Drenthe the dead were no longer added into a grave for ten thousand bodies, but were buried separately in a hole in the ground.

Schoonebeek used to be a peat-colony. Now only 600 hectare of peat and a small number of Saxon farms are left.

After the Second World War Schoonebeek received its fame due to the oil-extraction by the Netherlands Oil Company.

Today still Schoonebeek owns the most important oil-field in the Netherlands. The oil is extracted from the ground by pumping units and transported by train to the refinery in Pernis.

Water mill 'Singraven'

Water-wheel mills are very much older than the concept of windmills with sails. Especially at the eastern border of the Netherlands you can find these sources of environmentally friendly energy. This because here the rivers and brooks flow from higher to lower ground.

The water-wheel mill of Singraven is thought to have a ghost. Long ago a nun was bricked up behind a wall and its is said that she haunts the mill and there where her fateful castle once stood. Who will give her peace?

Singraven Castle

In the area known as the Achterhoek in the provence Gelderland, there are a large number of beautifully restored castles and manorials. You can find eight castles situated in and around the village of Vorden. The partly 16th century castle Ruurloo is surrounded by a park of at least 1.000 hectare.

Near Delden lies the Twickel property, with an estate bearing the same name. The original castle complex was built half way the 14th century with a moat around it. The estate has a large number of typical lengthy-home farms, often these houses had a room upstairs. The Weldam House is in the village of Kerspel Good (part of the Markelo city council).

   The nobleman's house stands proudly along the canal. Eggerich Ripperda commissioned a double beechen basement 'corps de logies' around 1560.

Ruurlo Castle   *Delden Castle*   *Twickel Castle*

Traffic in Giethoorn and the nearby Dwarsgracht still mostly travels over water. That is why it is nicknamed 'Venice of the North'.

Farm boats, canalboats and many other boats belonging to working people travel within the village. In the tourist season though you can hire one of about 400 so-called 'whisper boats' and too use the village canal.

The fleet of electronic punts replaced the ones which ran on petrol. Originally Giethoorn was a typical peat village that exported millions of squares of peat. When the peat supply was exhausted, the people of Giethoorn changed over to cattle farming. Then stables and storage barns were built behind the small peat houses. The view in the village changed as all the new buildings with their thatched roofs resembles a blanket of camelhair. In those days using reed for roofs was cheap. Now having a thatched roof is very expensive.

Dwarsgracht

Actually, this area provides the best reed for thatched roofs in Europe. The water in and around Giethoorn is very clear and therefore has much fish. Twenty-three different kinds of fish have been seen swimming there. That is why many restaurants always have eel and pike-perch on their menu.

Another phenomena in the region are the many duck decoys. It used to be that each season ten thousands of ducks were caught this way, to end up on someone's plate. There is a Dutch expression 'de pijp uitgaan' (leaving by the pipe), and it refers to this way of catching ducks.

There are a few very remarkable museums in Giethoorn. There is also a very old (150 years) and famous pub called Fanfare. It was renamed after the film made by a Dutch film maker Bert Haanstra in 1958.

Binnenpad

The fortress Blokzijl used to be located directly along the Zuiderzee. In 1942 the dykes of the North East polder were closed causing the small harbour town to be no longer near open water. Yet each year about 20.000 ships and boats pass through the picturesque lock. Surrounding the inner harbour you can see very nice looking old merchant houses.

Around 1650 many ship owners from Amsterdam, Hoorn and Enkhuizen moved to Blokzijl. The beautiful tower you can see in the sky-line belongs to the first protestant church built in the Netherlands. In 1997/1998 the church was thoroughly restored and now is also used for cultural activities.

Lock   *View over the harbour*

The whole town of Blokzijl is listed as state monuments. This town forms the gate-way to the 'De Weerribben', a National Park (owned by State Forestry) and to the Nature Reserve 'De Wieden' (owned by a Natuurmonumenten Association). The area is almost 15.000 hectare of protected countryside without any 'horizon pollution'.

Blokzijl and surrounding area are well known for good places to have a meal.

Light House

The fishing village of Urk used to be an island in the Zuiderzee until this became IJsselmeer in 1932 (see Afsluitdijk 46).
In 1942 Urk became connected to the provinces Friesland and Overijssel by dykes. The water between the dykes was pumped away to leave land now known as the Noordoost polder.
Urk commands a IJsselmeer fleet and a North Sea fleet of ships, boats. Their North Sea fleet is the largest in the Netherlands. Their main catches are sole and plaice.

The former islanders are a close community who treat Sunday as a holy day of rest and expect visitors to do the same. The old building with its green painted wooden gables is very picturesque. The Dutch Reformed Church dates back to 1786. The bell is from 1461.

It is a fascinating sight as the fleet sails out on a Monday. There is always something to see at the local shipyards.
During the summer many watersport lovers cross over the IJsselmeer between Urk and the other side. From which side of the water can you feast on fish more? Urk still is an independent municipal.

Shipyard

'Batavia'

The Flevo polder lies 4.30 metre under sea-level and became dry land in 1957. It is mostly covered with reed sowed from seed dropped from an aeroplane. Flevoland has enough space and wind for the windmill park that generates enough power to supply 10.000 inhabitants of electricity. The park is still under expansion.

It is on this completely new land of Netherlands the old trade of shipbuilding was revived. At a shipyard near Lelystad the ship that travelled to the East-Indies called the Batavia was rebuilt. It was the largest ship ever built in those times and able to carry provisions for 200 to 300 men and 160 foot long.

Nieuw Land Poldermuseum

All around the shipyard several different old crafts were situated. A wood-carvery, rig-workshop for the 22 kilometre rope and a sails-loft preparing 1.180 square metres of sail. The only crafts that did not position themselves near the ship were the blacksmith and the company that cast the 24 canons, together weighing 30 tons. The building of the V.O.C. ship 'De Seven Provinces' is still taking place.

Windmill Park

Windpark Irene Vorrink heeft dit jaar al voor ▮▮▮▮▮ huishoudens NATUURSTROOM geleverd.

Vispoort

The street plan of the historic centre of Elburg looks like a chess board, after the Roman castellum. In 1233 Elburg was granted town-rights. Elburg was moved and rebuilt between 1392 and 1396, as it kept flooding on the original spot.

Vispoort Bridge

On either side of the impressive wall tower 'the Vispoort' you can see parts of the wall which was built around the town. There are still canon vaults and 16th century casemates to be seen. Particularly interesting are the pavements laid in white and black pebbles.

Agnites Monastery

Vispoort

The Weigh House in Deventer was built between 1528 and 1531. The building has four corner towers with banisters around that give it a gothic look.
The weighing scales were situated on the ground floor. The rooms on the floors above were used as Guard facilities.

Museum 'de Waag'

Panorama from the IJssel

The town has a long reputation for producing a long small spiced gingerbread: the Deventer Koek. There is a silver cup that the cake-backers guild awarde to this 'koek'. The first time was in 1659 and keeping this cup is considered important.

The many 16th, 17th and 18th century gables determine the atmosphere of the town. Also the 15th century Lebuinus Church, the three fortress towers and remainders of the city wall near the IJssel are very much worth visiting.

Bolwerks Mill (1863)

In the year 1482 the small town of Bronkhorst was granted town rights, but it did not enjoy the expected growth. That is why it is now the smallest town in the Netherlands. It has been completely restored to its former glory.

It is possible to relive the Middle Ages as you walk through the small cobbled streets. There are little antique shops, a lovely picturesque town square and many other interesting sights. There is a 14th century castle-chapel. The interior has some interesting plates showing different coats of arms and a organ in a cabinet.

Dutch Reformed Chapel

The farmhouses in the IJssel area are mostly typical hall-houses in a T-shape. They differ from other types of farmhouses which can be seen in this part of the Netherlands. In these farmhouses the large doors of the storage building were not put back, but the wagons with the harvest did stay dry covered by the 'overstek', a overhanging part of the roof situated just above the exit.

Castle road

Drogenaps Tower

A very interesting historical fact can be seen in the Saint Walburgs Church, a very old library. This library held 400 books which together were of tremendous value. Learned men from all over Europe came to this church-library where the books were collected by the clergymen.

Berkel Gate   *Lion House*

In 1300 B.C. a stone wall was built around the town. The wealthy merchants built many beautiful houses and religious buildings with spires. The town then was nick-named Zutphania Turrita (the spiral city).

The old city walls are almost completely in tact as well as the very old city centre. The centre was built in the shape of a quarter circle. The Green market, Wood market and Seed market is where 900 years ago weekly markets were held. Now it is prohibited for any motorised vehicles.

Agnite Convent

Old dining room

'The Versailles of the North' is what the beautiful gardens in Baroque style belonging to the palace Het Loo (no longer used as a palace) are called. The gardens are a pleasure to look at with the fountains, terraces, English parterres, statues and water pieces.

It has been the largest and best prepared restoration ever in the Netherlands. So now the complete complex has been brought back to the original state in which it was when King-Stadtholder William III lived there. Every later addition has been removed, especially those from the 20th century. Even the layer of plaster put up in the time of Lodewijk Napoleon had to be removed. He had called it the white palace in green.

Audience-chamber

With the status of Rijksmuseum the building is a monument with 300 years of history of the House of Orange-Nassau. The interior and detailed decoration of the rooms and halls in the main building as well as the four pavilions on either side illustrate how the Orange family have lived here.

The audience-chamber is a very impressive room. There is a drawing-room dedicated to King William III (in Neo-gothic style) and one to Queen Emma. After stepping down as monarch, Queen Wilhelmina moved to palace Het Loo and wanted to be called princess again. In her office you can see where she wrote her impressive memoirs 'Lonely but not alone'.

Library

The town hall of Doesburg was built in late gothic style and is one of the oldest in the country. The town hall stood in this location when Doesburg was granted town-rights in 1237. The building you can see now dates back from the 15th century and was built on exactly the same spot.

In front of the town hall stands the 'Blue Stone' that refers to the origins of the word 'lichte kooi' (light cage). A cage used to be placed on the stone in which women of easy virtue were spun round.

The Weigh House, also known as the High House Gelria, has always been the town's beer house. The oldest restaurant in the Netherlands is situated here since 1478.

Hospital hofje

The Weigh House   *Town hall*

Waal Bridge

Nijmegen, together with Maastricht and Utrecht, one of the oldest towns in the country. Only in these places it is still possible to find traces of Roman times.

Nijmegen is ideally situated along the river Waal and the Maas-Waal Canal. It is therefore an important town for all waterway traffic travelling from Rotterdam to the hinterland in the Ruhr area.

Nicolaas Chapel

Barbarossa ruins

In the 8th century Charles the Great built a Palts on the Valkhof, on top of the foundations of a much older Merovingish palace.

Nijmegen then became the centre of rule over the northern part of his kingdom. In 1047 the Palts was destroyed. Frederik van Barbarossa rebuilt it again in late Roman style in 1155, but the building was demolished around 1800. After demolition, only the Saint Maartens Chapel remained. Now this is Barbarossa Castle.

The most important remainders of the 15th century stronghold are the Kronenburger Tower and the Belvedère.

Weigh House

Most of the houses in Thorn were built in the 18th century. This little white town looks like time has just stopped.
Many of the street have been paved with stones from the river Maas.

Here and there mosaics have been made into the pavements. Many white houses line these streets of a town that once was the capital of a miniature kingdom. The abbot to the Abbey reported only to the German Emperor. The Abby experienced its hight of wealth in the 18th century, which can be noticed as interior of the church is baroque.

The gothic styled Abbey church has a west wing built in Roman style and a 19th century tower.

Ruins of Valkenburg Castle

A ruin is all that is left of the Valkenburg Castle, but it is a very impressive one. It is the only real highest stronghold in our country. Especially the remains of the 13th century Knights' Hall with its pointed arches speaks to the imagination.

Passing through the Velvet cave you come to the passages under the castle ruins. Valkenburg Castle was blown up by troops from Holland who conquered it from the French. Valkenburg fortress posed a great threat to the nearby Maastricht that in those day still was controlled by the State.

The Spanish Leenhof, built by the Spaniards in 1661 is very interesting. First is was used as a House of Justice and later the Stadtholder used it to live in. The parish church is dedicated to the holy Saint Nicolas and the holy Barbara. Patron saints for travellers and miners. The 'French Mill' used to be in hands of a French family, but now the grain mill is a museum.

Schaloen Castle

Genhoes Castle

The 'French Mill'

Set in the hilly countryside with its valley where the river Geul can flow without dykes, Limburg is the most un-Dutch provence of the Netherlands. Limburg is where marl comes from. About ninety percent of the countryside in southern Limburg is not allocated to private owners. Small agricultural fields and meadows give a very attractive view of the countryside.

People have farmed for a very long time (4000 B.C.) and professional farming is no different. Although the people here sound foreign the land has always been a part of the Netherlands. It is better to visit one of the many monuments yourself than to read about en of them, as it is a joy to discover so much interesting yourself.

Saint Servaas Bridg

The oldest town gate in the Netherlands can of course be found in one of the oldest towns. Maastricht definitely has the oldest bridge with and even older river flowing under it. The St. Servaas Bridge dates back to 1280 - 1298. A spectacular view of the river Maas and Maastricht can be seen from the highest point on the bridge.

At the end of the 14th century Bishop St. Servatius transferred the bishop's seat to Maastricht, Then it was called Trajectum (Trajectum ad Mosam, meaning ford across the Maas). There are more buildings in town named after this man. The St. Servaas Basilica is one of the largest and most beautiful roman churches in the Netherlands. The absolute showpiece in the St. Servaas is the treasure-chamber is the shrine in which the relics of the holy Servatius are kept, the so-called Distress Chest. The holy object made with gold and precious stones was taken on processions through the streets of Maastricht in times of distress.

St. Servaas Church

Helpoort

Vrijthof   *Jeker House* ▲

Another important roman church building can be found on the Vrijthof, the large town square. This is the 'Onze Lieve Vrouwe Church', also known as Slevrouwe. It is a very popular church as numerous miracles have taken place here.

Art historians appreciate the Slevrouwe for a different reason. Its interior has many magnificent columns, of which the 'Heimo' is world famous.

Onze Lieve Vrouwe Church

Evoluon

Eindhoven does not look the old town that is actually is. Most of the obvious monuments are less that 100 years old. One example is the 'Evoluon', a spectacular building designed by Dr. Kalft that resembles a flying saucer. This exhibition building is dedicated to modern technology.

The Abbe Museum was erected by the cigar manufacturer Henri van Abbe and is well known for its important collection of modern art from Picasso, Kandinski and Mondriaan to name but a few.

Van Abbe Museum

Opwettens Water mill

Situated near the town of Eindhoven you can see the Opwettens water mill. This mill set the scene for a painting by the famous Dutch painter Vincent van Gogh.

Colls Water mill

In the centre of the town of 's-Hertogenbosch are the most beautiful buildings, streets and alleyways. These are all around the 'Markt' and the 'Parade', the worldly and the spiritual hart of the city respectively. The town hall from the outside seems very overbering with its classicist gable, but inside there are the most lovely Gobelin tapestries and murals.

Dieze

Spherical houses

The Zwanebroedershuis (Swan Brothers House) was built in 1846 and still every year the large group of the Brotherhood of the Swan gather here to enjoy the traditional meal of swan. The Brotherhood's main activity is charity.

The fifty very unusual modern spherical houses are very appropriately been built in the 'Bulb field' area. These houses were designed by the architect Krey-amp.

St. Jan Cathedral

The fortification that can been seen here is a reconstruction of the situation at the end of the 16th century. This was when the small town needed to protect itself from the Spaniards. In the 17th and 18th century Heusden's economy was thriving on having a garrison in town. It lost its strategic significance when (it lay on the border between the provinces Holland and Brabant) the southern part of the Netherlands was added to create the larger new Kingdom of the Netherlands. The fortifications were dismantled and Heusden became poor.

Like many cities built in the Middle Ages, Heusden was designed and built at the same time. Therefore the town has a clear infrastructure. Standard mills were placed on the bastions, the same situation as in 1649.

Fish auction

Bird's eye view of Heusden

Ramparts with Standard mill

There used to a castle in Old Heusden, but it was destroyed by the Spaniards in 1589. It was rebuilt at a later time, but now only gatehouse from 1688 remains.

View of the Harbour

Panorama from the Powder Tower

This fortress was probably built between 1357 and 1368 by Dirk Loef van Horne. In 1576 a rampart (wall) was created surrounding the castle, later these became part of the fortress. Not far from the castle stands the round powder tower and annex buildings. This is all that remains of the fortress entrance.

After the Second World War the castle was renovated extensively and now it is a museum. Special events are sometimes held here.

See-through

Loevestein used to be a state prison. William II incarcerated Hugo the Great and members of the Holland anti-stadtholders regency party there. Jacob the Witt, lord mayor of Dordrecht, was one of them. After his death the prisoners were released and their honour restored.

Courtyard

Bouvigne Castle

Spaniardsgat

Onze Lieve Vrouwekerk

Breda is a very diverse town, and the centre of the region for not only industrial reasons. It has many cultural and recreational facilities. 'Het Turfschip' is a congress and exhibition centre.

Breda is surrounded by fabulous forests which gives it a lovely entrance to the town. The Roman Catholic Church definitely left its mark on this town. The Onze Lieve Vrouwekerk is an interesting place to visit. The late gothic Basilica is impressive because it has the highest tower (97 metres) in North Brabant and the fact that the Roman Catholic Church chose Breda for the Bishop's seat in 1853.

Begijnhof

The Royal Military Academy is housed in the Breda Castle, and has been since 1828. Originally building started in 1350, but it was not finalized as a castle in Renaissance style until the 17th century
The Begijnhof from 1535 has luckily been spared.

Breda Castle

Berghen op ten Zoom was a 14th century harbour village where trade, fishing and a strategic point along the Schelde made it what it is. The Theodorus Harbour with 500 hectare of docks is reasonably important as much anchovies, oysters and mussels are brought in here.

Town Hall   *St. Gertrudis Church*

Bergen op Zoom is mainly an industrial town. Till 1747, the invincible stronghold was part of a Marquisate. The Markieshof is a reminder of those days. This late-gothic palace and homes for the gentlemen of Bergen op Zoom now house cultural buildings with the historic museum for example.

The St. Geertrudis church is a fine example of 15th century traditional brabant gothic architecture. The wooden tower was added after rebuilding in 1750.

Markiezenhof

This building is popularly called the 'Pepper shaker'. To spend a night in the oldest hotel in Holland must come to Bergen op Zoom. The establishment next to the historic home 'The Elephant' and town hall is still in use.

Prisoners Gate

Yerseke is well known for mussel and oyster cultivation along the coast. Yerseke has been an important centre for the cultivation of these sea-delicatessens for over a century. Oysters are produced in large crates that are collected in oyster tanks. Mussel-seed is divided equally over the large mussel tanks.

Harbour

Oyster tanks

Mussels grow 'naturally' and hardly move. Oyster cultivation seemed to be in danger for a while as plans for closing the Eastern Schelde completely were being discussed. Luckily a half-open tidal dam was built ensuring the future of cultivation. Severe winters can detrimental to oyster production. Gales have the same effect on mussels. Yerseke has a long history for this delicious seafood.

Traditional costume in Zeeland

Westkapelle Light House

Walcheren is the best known island in Zeeland although it has been connected to South-Beverland by the Sloedam since 1871. Whether Wal-acra means 'large field' or whether the island was named after the King of the Vikings Walcherius, one thing is certain Walcheren is one large field.

All the towns and villages seem to have a connection with the sea. Domburg is an international popular seaside resort. The abbots of Middelburg built their pleasure-house: Westhove Castle. The surrounding area is nature reserve.

Westhove Castle

On the south coast of Walcheren and at the mouth of the Wester-schelde lies Vlissingen, birthplace of Michiel de Ruyter. His statue stands at the top of the sea-front that is named after him. The Stedelijk Museum have, the 'large wheel' and the 'blue checkered blouse' in which he is said to have stood during his travels, on display.

Michiel de Ruyter

The 17th century made Vlissingen into a war-port. Already trade, fishing, departure for boats leaving for the Cape and slave-trade were the main sources of income.

Vlissingen is a very popular coastal resort with nice beaches with a nice sea-front along the south western coast. There are dunes and a forrest Nollebos. Dutch and Belgian pilot-services are located at the modern container harbour. It is the sixth largest harbour city in the Netherlands with 30.000 square metres of storage space in 8 separate harbours. The Royal Navy has a small base here. The High School of Navigation is located here too.

The Arsenal Museum

Campveerse toren

The small town of Campen one could only reach by ferry, but in the 14th century a tidal wave washed it away. The place were the ferry left to travel to Campen became known as Veere. Veere was located on the Lords van Borssele's property. Their castle was nearby. Wolvert VI, one of the lords, married a Scottish princess in 1444.

Following this liaison a lively trade in wool started between Scotland and Veere. At ome point in time it became only possible to import the Scottish wool via Veere as they had sole stowing rights. In turn the Scottish colony enjoyed numerous privileges, facilities and a Scottish house (actually two houses) for themselves called 'The lamb'. In 1545 Veere became part of a Marquisate that belonged to the House of Orange and so the Queen was the marquess of Veere and Vlissingen.

Windmill 'The Cow'

The gigantic Onze-Lieve-Vrouwe Church and the eye-catching high tower of the town hall are dominant for the small town. The tower was built in renaissance style as it was build about 100 years later than the town hall, but the harmony between the two is just perfect.

On the gables are small statues which are copies made in the 1930's. They depict the Women of Borssele. The originals are on view in the Scottish Houses' museum.

Stadtholder and King William III was Marquis of Veere. His legacy are the lovely and valuable doorknobs to the great hall in the town hall and a portrait of himself.

View over the harbour

Town Hall

It is certain that the original stronghold was built to protect the population of Zeeland from the water and enemies. Not so certain is who the enemy was. Were the Vikings the enemy or did Viking King Harald have the flee-castle built? In the 10th century the Counts of Vlaanderen and Holland used it to create a fortification.

The set-up of the town is still clear visible on the street-plan of the centre of Middelburg. Middelburg became a prosperous merchant city. The great wealth was spent on large buildings such as the town hall and abbey. The master builders family Keldermans were commissioned to build the town hall and used the town hall in Brussels as their example. This resulted in glorious construction made with three wings, a tower with a carillon and a Choer tower. Albrecht Dührer called the chimes 'tower delightful' when he visited.

Spijker Bridge

St. Jorisdoelen

The Kloverniersdoelen and St. Jorisdoelen have the most beautiful gables. Kloverniers were the members of the citizen soldiery. Doelen is the name for the practice area of the 'Van de Edele Busse' guild. As gunpowder was to be stored at the doelen it had to be built on the outskirt of Middelburg. The gables of the St. Jorisdoelen show the patron in combat with a dragon.

The original abbey was much larger when the monks lived there. It is easy to understand that the abbey in Middelburg is unique in the Netherlands. The abbey consisted of two churches, a large tower rising 85 metres, a cloister and some courtyards. The marble mausoleum of the admirals Johan and Cornelius Evertsen born in Zeeland has been placed in the connection between the two churches. The mausoleum was the last large assignment of the sculpturer Rombout Verhulst.

The two heroes of the sea died in 1666 during the Second English War. Long John is the popular name for the tall and rare octagonal tower of the Koor church. Actually this nickname is a popular name for many other tall tower in the Netherlands. In the Middle Ages the number eight symbolized perfection and so the octagon was the symbol for a perfect town, the heavenly Jerusalem.

The Abbey

Storm Flood Barrier

Zeeland Bridge

A spokesman for the West-Brabant Water Board proclaimed 'It is our highest official priority to protect the population against drowning and flooding'. In February 1953 200.000 hectares of land flooded and 1835 people drowned in one night. To guarantee that this disaster would never happen again the Delta Plan was set up. It is an impressive and effective defence mechanism against the oldest enemy that the Netherlands has: water. The large complex of locks in the dam built right across the river Haringvliet plays a key role in the control of the water. It can be seen as 'the main tap in the Netherlands'.

The final defence in the battle against the liquid foe is the storm flood barrier built across the mouth of the Eastern Schelde. It is 9 kilometres long and is a tidal dam with steel lift gates that can be raised and lowered. It was extremely important that each foundation-mat and buttress were positioned exactly right, with only up to 25 centimetres leeway. It is considered a technical world miracle.

Brouwers Dam

North Harbour Gate ▶

South Harbour Gate ▶▶

Town Hall

North Harbour Gate

The exuberant renaissance tower of the town hall is absolutely unique. The gables are covered with portraits of Charles V and his son Filips. The carillon that used to decorate the tower is the oldest in the Netherlands and was replaced by more modern chimes in the 1920's. Peter van Gheyn had made the carillon around 1550-1554.

The South Harbour Gate and the North Harbour Gate formed the protection from all entrance roads from the east. It ensured the safety of the old harbour too. Along the old harbour a couple of very nice-looking houses from the Louis XV and Louis XVI period can be enjoyed.

Nobel Gate

Light House

Hellevoetsluis was dominated by the navy, as it was a naval base and a shipping harbour. In 1923 the navy moved away which meant the steady decline of fortress town. There are still traces of its rich naval past, such as the dry-dock used for the war fleet.

The town hall used to be home to the gentlemen of the Admiralty and dates back from around 1650.

Along the Eastern Quay you can see the Admiralty Warehouse built at the end of the 17th century. An old mill had to be demolished to make way for the fortress. Fortunately the round windmill 'De Hoop' from 1802 was spared and still mills grain.

Town Hall

Grote Church

Dordrecht lies where the river Merwede divides into the Old Maas and North. The Mallegat and Dordse Kil branches off there. Dordrecht is the oldest town of the original Holland provinces with perhaps one of the most picturesque harbour. The Grote Church or rather Onze Lieve Vrouwe Church has a tower from the 13th century. From the tower you have a fantastic view over the city with its many monuments and distant countryside and rivers.

Dordrecht has so many historical buildings and monuments that you do not know where to look first. The specifically Dordrecht type of making gables was started already in the 16th century. The upper floors have profiled arches.

There are still a few pilaster gables to be seen, such as on the 'De Onbeschaamde' (the impudent) house from the 17th century. Dordrecht has many gates, passages and courtyards with lovely views of the town. The Begijnhofpoort, the delicate Muntpoortje from 1555, the Oudemanhuispoort in baroque style and the lovely Arend Maartenshof-poort to name a few offer lovely insight into Dordrecht.

Merwede

Arend Maertenszhof (anno 1625)

Kuipers Harbour

Looking for the 'Stedenmaagd' (town virgin) you must look above the gate on the north side of the Groothoofd.

In 1930 Dordrecht started expanding its harbour area to enable larger and deeper ships to reach the town. During the Second World War the harbour was destroyed, but by 1948 it was rebuilt again.

Many large and important industrial companies are located at Dordrecht. Almost half of the Dordrecht population work in the industrial sector. After the industrial area 'the Maasvlakte' was completed, it meant that sea-shipping business was to be diverted to there. Dordrecht is still a very important harbour to the inland shipping and especially pusher-tugs.

*Kinderdijk
with night-
illuminations*

At the edge of the Alblasserwaard and near the industrial area of the Rijnmond lies Kinderdijk. Legend has it that during a flood a baby in a cradle floated ashore here while being kept in balance by a cat to prevent it from toppling over. There are no less than nineteen windmills that can be found here.

This legacy belongs on the World Heritage List of UNESCO. Much money is needed, as not all the windmills work and those that do, do not work enough to pay for back-maintenance.

The mills date back to 1740 and are good for between 200.000 and 300.000 tourists each year with almost as many photo- and video cameras.

Skating near the windmills

Euromast

The Euromast is situated on the Parkhaven in Rotterdam. It's total height is 185 metres. From the restaurant there is a fantastic view over the city and the mondial harbour. One of the many attraction is a ride on the Space Cabin. It also holds alternating exhibitions. The Euromast was built in 1960 with the Space-Tower added in 1970. It is a definite landmark for the Rotterdam.

Modern architecture has been able to develop itself in Rotterdam. Two of the latest exhibits of modern architecture are the cubical houses designed by Piet Blom and the Erasmus Bridge. The Erasmus Bridge is popularly known as 'The Swan'. Along the Coolsingel and on the Hofplein (square) you can find modern 'Skyscrapers' that reflect the old style of building. There is a shopping centre on the Lijnbaan. This large harbour town was ahead of its time already in 1898. It was then when the 'White House' was built. It stood 45 metres high and at that time was the highest building in Europe.

Leuve Harbour ❦   *Erasmus Bridge*

Cubical houses   St. Laurens Church ▶

Luckily there are still some picturesque spots in the town that remind one of the past. In and around the Old Harbour you find quaint sights. The Open Air Inland Shipping Museum has its home in the Old Harbour.

On the twenty-third floor of the (WTC) World Trade Center there is a Business Club with a bar and a lounge for members and their guests. The WTC library contains thousands of books and periodicals concerning 'trade'. The Wholesalers building is of an earlier date. This is a complex in which many companies have their offices. It has eight floors, is 220 metre long and 85 metres wide.

Hofplein   *The White House* ▶▶

Erasmus Bridge

World Trade Center

Euromast

It seems that this largest port in the world never sleeps. At night you can see the twinkling of lights in the high office buildings or bright lights that light up objects or buildings that look like art.

Europoort

Pernis

Maasvlakte

Especially at night Rotterdam is a dynamic city. The town and harbour give a fairy-like impression. On the Maasvlakte area, at the Europoort and in the Pernis area work continues day and night. The dynamics of these places can be felt when you see the millions of lights, cranes with their spotlights and the many ships that come and go. Rotterdam's pulse beats every day of the year, every minute of the day.

New Waterway

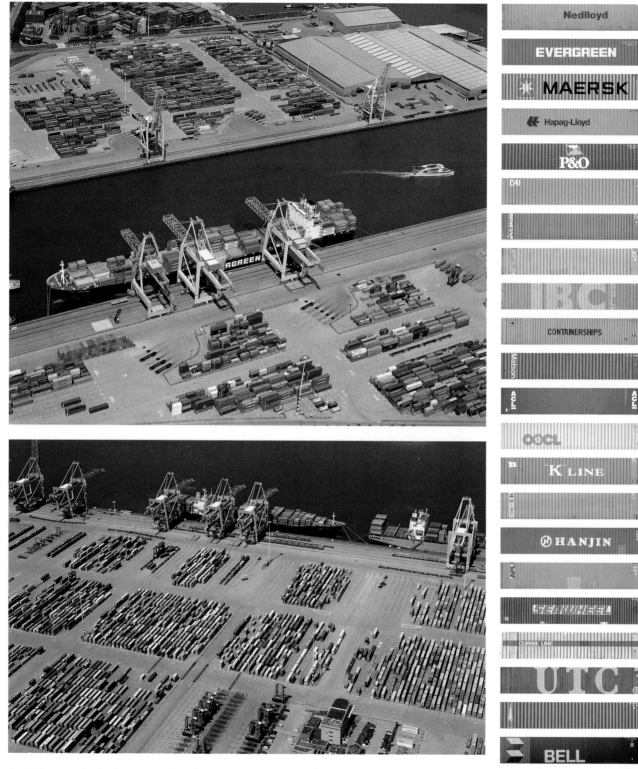

In 1957, when the harbour was undergoing enormous expansion the name Europoort ('euro gate') was chosen. With this name they want to indicate that Rotterdam intended to be the 'Gateway to Europe'.

From 1963, and now still Rotterdam can call itself the biggest port and storage area in the world. Rotterdam has invested a lot of money and space for trans-shipment facilities for containers. It wants to compete with the Far East. The largest container ships can easily be unloaded at any of the terminal on the Maasvlakte.

Pernis

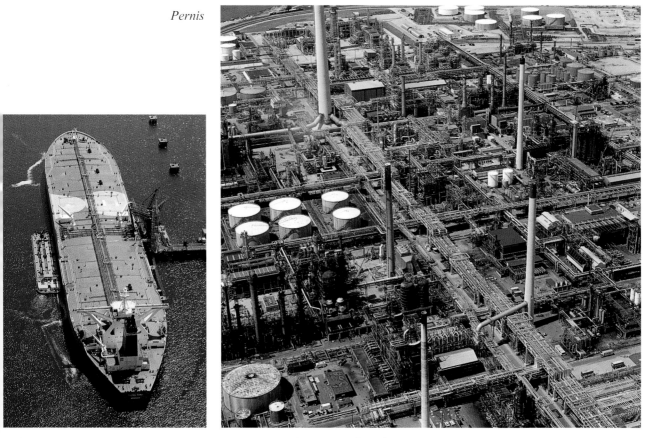

Waal Harbour

Standardizing the sizes of all containers has made loading and unloading easier.

Mainly cars, especially Japanese cars, are unloaded in the Brittania Harbour which lies behind the Caland Bridge in the Botlek dock area. Ships carrying cars can be identified by the extra high decks that make them very sensitive to wind.

In Pernis and on the Maasvlakte the oil refineries dominate the type of transport. The Petroleum Harbours expanded tremendously in numbers and in size, since 1936.

Waal Harbour specializes more in the unloading of general cargo. Much is loaded 'on the stream' which means directly into inland ships.

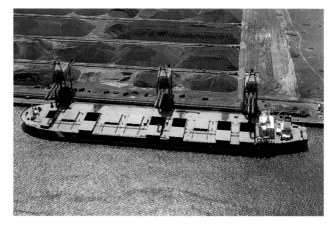

Mississippi Harbour

Barrier closed

At the mouth of the Nieuwe Waterweg lies Hoek van Holland. This is the home port for the ferry service to Harwich in England. It forms an important link in the export of agricultural products from the nearby Westland farmland.

Hoek van Holland is a divided village that used to be part of The Hague. In 1914 it was added to the greater Rotterdam council. This council is called 'Rijnmond'.

   The waterway connects Rotterdam and Europoort and was dug between 1866 and 1872.

Side view from the south side of the Nieuwe Waterweg

Barrier closed

One of the most remarkable pieces of Dutch workmanship in gaining control over water is the system that can close off the Nieuwe Waterweg completely, whenever a storm surge or high spring tide occurs. The final part of the Delta Works was put into operation by Queen Beatrix on 10th May 1996. Now millions of people in the provence South-Holland are protected from the North Sea. A model of the storm flood barriers can be seen in the miniature town Madurodam in The Hague.

Hoek of Holland is the nearest seaside resort with beautiful beaches for the inhabitants of Rotterdam and surrounding areas. Shipping apparatus, pilotage and rescue services are all located here too.

Westland is the area behind the dunes between The Hague and the mouth of the river Maas. After a few adjustments this land is very suitable for horticulture. It is ideally located so near The Hague and the towns along the Maas. The products can be freshly delivered here. As the Westland is near the North Sea the temperature in winter is slightly higher than elsewhere in the country. In summer the sea-breeze is cooling.
At the turn of the century the growers decided collectively to grow their products in glasshouses. Their decision was based on not wanting to be completely dependant on the climate. After the glasshouses were built the landscape changed into a immense glass carpet.

In these glasshouses the temperature, humidity, oxygen, nutrients and disease control can be monitored perfectly. Almost everything can be controlled except for the most important factor: sunlight. The Westland growers need to 'catch' as much sunlight and warmth from the sun as possible for their 'Glass town'.

Lettuce

Mostly vegetables and flowers are grown in the glasshouses. It is often cheaper to import fruit from abroad. Chrysanthemums, originally a plant that blooms in autumn, now will flower all year round. They are the most cultivated plant in the Westland.

There is a 1.400 hectare area of glasshouses with just ornamental plants. The flower auction is a co-operation and owned by 3.000 members. Six hundred people work at the auction which has a turn-over of 1 milliard guilders.

In the beginning of cultivation under glass, the glasshouses resembled a long row of windows just above the ground. Nowadays glass warehouses are built to make optimal use of the sunlight.

Traditional vegetables such as lettuce, cucumber, endives and spinach are grown, but lately also more challenging crops are cultivated.

Glasshouses by night

Many of the growers have replaced the original soil with soil containing more nutrients. This form of cultivation, called substrate cultivation, decrease chances of disease and less water is needed.

Town Hall

Delft is well known for several reasons: Delft blue pottery, work-place of the painter Vermeer and being a typical Dutch town (in comparison to size of the town there are very many canals).
Delft also has a less than perfect history. The 'Codfish' town sur-rendered to the Count Albrecht van Beieren, there was a fire that destroyed a large part of the city in 1536 and in 1572 the prote-stants occupied the town just after the town of Den Briel fell.

Oostpoort

William of Orange made his home in the Prinsenhof in Delft. This is where the 'Father of the Fatherland' was shot by Balthazar Gerardts. The mausoleum is in the New Church. On the mauso-leum a work made from marble and touchstone shows the prince with a dog at his feet. The dog stopped eating after its master died and wanted to die too. In the transept and the chorus leaded win-dows have been made to commemorate our William of Orange.

Vrouwenregt

⏶ *Covered meat market*

In 1381 there was a miraculous appearance of the Virgin Maria. It was decided to build a wooden church on that spot. Later it was replaced by the current New Church.

Building on the tower designed to be the tallest in the Netherlands began in 1396. The tower, 108 meters high, was even taller than the steep top on the Dom in Utrecht. It took a hundred years to complete the tower. The Onze-Lieve-Vrouwe Chapel was added in 1510.

New Church

's-Gravenhage is the correct name for the town that holds the seat for our parliamentary democracy in the Netherlands. The Hague is the more commonly used name. The Hague is the capital of the provence South-Holland. Queen Beatrix lives here, her office is in the palace on the Noordeinde is near to her home.

Standing in front of Noordeinde palace it seems that one of her ancestors is standing guard on his horse. The palace used to be called the Old Hof. There are more palaces in The Hague, 'Het Lange Voorhout' and the (previously) Kneuterdijk Palace.

Huis ten Bosch was built by Frederik Hendrik and was mainly used for representative purposes. In winter the Hofvijver (pond) entertains the many ice skaters.

Opening of Parliament

Noordeinde Palace

Binnenhof, Parliament building

n summer often groups wanting to catch he attention of the media will stage a manifestation here. In the centre, behind he Hofvijver lies the Mauritshuis which is now a museum. The small tower to the eft is the office of the Dutch Prime Minis- er. The chamber of the Lower House is located in a very modern building.

On the third Tuesday of September Queen Beatrix opens parliament. This is done in the Great Hall of the Binnenhof. Her Majesty arrives in the Golden Coach which was once a gift to the Royal family from the population of Amsterdam. The splendour usually has lots of 'Orange Sun' and many royalists come to see.

Hofvijver (pond)

The Peace Palace plays an important role internationally. Often world leaders gathe- red here to consider solutions for conflicts elsewhere in the world. The International Court of Law is located here too, as well as the Academy for International Law.

The Hague likes to be seen as an open city, a focus point for art, business and diplomacy. Regularly international con- gresses and exhibitions are held here.

Peace Palace

Set of windmills in winter

This could look like a typical Dutch christmas card: the three windmills forming a working unit in the wintry landscape. These can be found in the Driemanspolder near Wilsveen. This is between Leidschendam and Zoetermeer. The dam that used to be there has been replaced by a lift-lock in the river Vliet.

Songs have been written about nice girls skating on the Vliet. Where else would it be possible to come into contact with the opposite sex as easily as on the ice? Even in summer the area is pretty romantic, sitting in a boat in between the reeds or even fishing along the water-side.

Wind is the force behind the turning of the sails of the windmill. Depending on how much wind there is the sails are covered completely or partially. The miller must make sure the mill is positioned 'into the wind' by pushing it round using a special mechanism. Before steam engines came into use, about 9000 windmills were in use. Steam and electricity brought down 8000 of them. The 1000 we have left are treasured dearly. There are many different types of Dutch mills.

The oldest tower mill (1450) can still be seen in Gelderland and Limburg. The hollow post mills, as seen below, have interesting working technic. A hollow post mill is a mill with a water-wheel, a small trunk and the bottom part shaped like a pyramid. There are many of this kind of mill in the region of Leidschendam and Leiden.

Scheveningen has beautiful broad beaches and a seemingly endless sea. There is a fabulous view down over the beaches from the promenade that is higher up. The fishing village is next to The Hague. Actually it is part of The Hague municipality, but the people of Scheveningen do definitely not consider themselves 'The Haguers'. Characters differ too much. Scheveningen has a modern fish auction where Scheveningen trawlers (used to be luggers) come to auction their fish.

Till 1904 the fishing boats were pulled onto the beaches. Ships with a keel had their home port in Vlaardingen. At present Scheveningen has three harbours. The first and second inner harbours are for professional ships and the third is a very luxurious harbour for yachts.

The light house looks somewhat majestic and the light can be seen for miles. It shows the sea ships the way home. Flag day is a very colourful tradition. This day is celebrated when the first Dutch new herring is brought in.

Scheveningen Pier

The worldly seaside resort has much to offer: a Casino, the Kurhaus and also a pier. On the pier there is a children play area in the form of an island, a hall that can accommodate at least 1.000 people and a large tower from which to enjoy the view. There used to be a wooden pier which was opened by Queen Wilhelmina in 1901. This burned down in 1942. In 1961 Prince Bernard opened the current promenade pier. Since then several modernisations have taken place.

Light House

Both the town hall and the weigh house have gables made made of natural stone. The sculpture work was done by Bartholomeus Eggers.

Along the side of the river Gouwe market was held in the 17th century 'fish temple'.

The word 'Gouda' used as an adjective refers to not only the full-cream cheese, but also to the traditional pipe made of white stone, to Gouda pottery and of course Gouda candles.

The town hall built in late-gothic style and dominates the triangular market place was erected between 1448 and 1459. The use of natural stones for the outside of the building gives it an un-Dutch look.

There have been a number of changes to the building over the years. In 1518 the dilapidated cellar was replaced by the covered meat market and the steps to the entrance were added in 1603.

Town Hall

The dormers to the town hall date back to
1626 and at the end of the 17th century
the additions were a cover for the flight of
steps, three chimneys and a scaffold at the
rear side of the building.

Inner Harbour Museum   *Weigh House*

Other type of stone was used for the towers when they were
replaced in 1880. After the war a renovation of most of the building except for the scaffold, flight of steps and the dormers.

Cheese Market

People are now married in what used to be the Lord Mayor's
Room. It has carpeted walls from the 17th century and Gouda
patroness on the mantlepiece.

Toll House

Hooglandse Church

Kooren Bridge

Academy Rapenburg

Hartebrug Church

The citadel in Leiden is a fine example of a fashionable castle. It is a castle built on an artificial hill. In 1151 the earl of Holland commissioned it to be built with a one meter thick wall around it. In 1581 the university moved into the old conventual church which had always belonged to Dominican nuns. Behind the Academy, the main building, lies the Hortus Botanicus. The Hortus, as it is generally called, has always had strong ties with the university. A herb garden from 1587 has been reconstructed on part of the old castle wall. The greenhouse was designed by Daniël Marot (1744).

Morsch Gate

Near the Academy you can find the Bibliotheca Thysiana. There is the legacy of the 17th century lawyer Johannes Thysius. The small Dutch classicistic building built in 1655 still contains its inventory and a book press from that time. For safe keeping some of the more important works are kept in the university library.

Most of places of interest in Leiden are in the western part of the town, within the bounds of the long and winding moats. A fine example is the old mill, De Valk (The Falcon). Near there you can see the Lakenhal (Cloth Hall). In the 14th and 15th century Leiden had a flourishing cloth industry.

Windmill 'De Put' (The Well)

For a very long time the cloth made in Leiden competed with the cloth made in Florence. After 1500 the English started to weave their own wool and it became harder and less profitable to find sources.

Besides the Academy and the libraries there is one more educationally characteristic building in Leiden: the Latin School. It was erected in 1431, renovated in 1600 and was used as a secondary grammar school till well into the 19th century.

In the past several great scholars have presented their knowledge in Leiden. An excellent example is the linguist Josephus Justus Scaliger (1540 - 1609) who came to Leiden to found the science of comparative linguistics. He spoke French, German, Italian, Greek, Arabic, Hebrew, Armenian, Syrian, Persian, Turkish and off course Latin. One of his pupils, Heusius, wrote his teacher's epitaph. He too was a well known linguist. The mausoleum of the medic Herman Boerhave (1762) located in the Pieter's Church is proof that the town of Leiden honoured its scholars. Boerhave was not only a medical graduate, but also a graduate in theology, philosophy and maths.

Stadstimmerwerf

When one says 'Lisse' they often mean 'Tulip time in Holland'. Almost 2000 years ago the whole region was peat-soil and dunes near a shallow river mouth. As the water could not flow into the sea, the ground grew superfluous vegetation that in turn created layers of peat-soil. People dug the top layers of the peat by hand and were left with soil which is a mixture of peat, clay and sand. This appeared to be very much suitable for the cultivation of flower bulbs. To the south of Lisse there is a robust half round tower ''t Huys Dever'. There is nothing else left of the castles in the region from the Middle Ages.

The property Keukenhof near Lisse holds a famous flower exhibition each year. Hundred of thousands of people from all over the world come to see it.

It is not surprising that the original castle Haar was destroyed by the 'Kabeljouwen'. The lord of the castle and the mayor of Utrecht, Dirk van Zuylen, used the fort as their base for the plundering of the surrounding countryside.

In 1892 a start was made on rebuilding the castle and the result is an old fashioned fairy castle. It has round corner towers, it is surrounded by water and has beautiful gardens and park. The architect Cuypers and landscape gardener Copijn wanted 12 hectare extra to be added to make it an even 500 hectare. The village De Haar was in the way of this plan and was therefore moved to another location. Luckily the village consisted of only 5 houses. The new building style used for the village was inspired by the castle. Professionally built houses made from bricks and shutters in the colours of the noble family.

The area around the castle can be divided into three parts:
1 A combination of baroque gardens with other shapes.
2 The Northern Park, which is a mix of baroque with English gardens.
   A 'Grand Canal' that is enclosed by crooked paths.
3 The Southern Park, a traditional English garden.

To get a proper idea of what the design would look like, many trees from all over the provence were dug up, including their roots, and transported by 'Mallejan'. The creation of the gardens and parks came to life with the help of the horses pulling carts doing most of the work.

Hall

The interior of the originally 15th century castle De Haar is as impressive as the exterior. Most items are from different style periods. It is possible to wander through this fairy-tale world because the castle as well as the grounds can be visited in the summer.

Ball Room

Library

Dining Hall

Dom Tower

In the 10th and 11th century it was customary for the German emperor, who ruled over Utrecht, to appoint the bishops himself. In those days, the bishop was more a stadtholder than a spiritual leader.

Emperor Koenraad died in 1039 during a celebration of Whitsuntide. His hart and intestines were taken out and put on the chorus of the Dom Church. The rest of the corps was then transported to the Dom in Spiers. His son and heir Henry III together with bishop Bernhold decided to create a cross made from churches. The Dom Church in Utrecht, with Koenraads hart, would be in the centre. This was as a homage to his father.

In the east the Pieters Church was built, to the north the Jans Church and in the south the Paulus abbey. Around 1058 a start was made on building the Maria Church that was to be at the 'foot' of the cross. Building was not completed until the 12th century.

The Dom, Salvator, Pieters, Jans and Maria Churches are the five main churches or capital churches of Utrecht.

Capital churches were to most powerful land owners. The land surrounding the capital church was immune, invincible and often surrounded by a wall or moat. They resembled spiritual republics within the town.

Old Canal

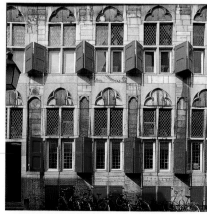

Eventually the bishop had to hand over quite a lot of his power and influence to the guilds. These 21 unions of colleagues compelled craftsmen to join. The guilds were also responsible for the town's defences. Each guild was responsible for a part of the defence, this was called a 'slag' (a beat). When the moat froze over each guild had to break the ice.

Zoudebalch

When bishop Adriaan Floriszoon returned from Spain around 1518, he said that the house he wanted to live in was a gift from God himself and he wanted to live in it more than any other house in Utrecht. In 1522 he was chosen to become pope and moved to Rome where he died in 1923. The house he referred to in Utrecht never actually became his home, but was named 'Pope House'. Between 1814 and 1954 it was the official residence of the governor. Since 1954 and parts of it are used for representative purposes by the Queen's Commissioner.

Pope House

Following the 300 years of the Union of Utrecht celebrations held in 1879 it was decided that a sculpture would be erected of the brother of the prince: Jan van Nassau. In 1883 the statue was unveiled by King William III. It is located in front of a small (neo-gothic) gate that leads to the cloister of the Dom and in front of the main church.

University Academy

For centuries there were several wells in Utrecht. Over the years pumps were built over these wells. Up till the 19th century people used these pumps for their water supply.

The most important pump was the one at the Mariaplaats. The water from this well regarded, so much even that in Amsterdam you could buy the water from Utrecht.

Old Canal

Shipyard

Along the river Eem that flows into the Eem Lake you will find Spakenburg. This village still upholds a number of old traditions. Smoked eel competitions are held each year and they have the special Fishery Days.

Especially the old and traditional crafts in and around the shipyards are an attraction.

You can watch how ships are built and restored on the Botter dock. To accommodate tourists many of the female population wear their traditional costume which is typical for Spakenburg with flowered stiff collar.

Traditional Costume

The men's traditional costume is black with a white and nay striped blouse with yellow clogs. It is well worth visiting 't Vurhuus, the Traditional Costume and Fishery Museum. Spakenburg forms a council together with Bunschoten, Eemdijk and Zevenhuizen. That is the reason for the letters BU (Bunschoten) on the ships in Spakenburg.

View of the harbour

Panorama over Naarden

Marksmen

Fortress wall

Town Hall

Perhaps, no definitely, Naarden is the best preserved fortress town in the Netherlands. The still existing fortifications were built between 1675 and 1685 by builder of fortresses: Adriaan Dortsman. The Vesting Museum (Fortress Museum) is located in one of the bastions. Archery is still active in Naarden. The town hall dates back from 1601 and has many interesting features. It was built in Renaissance style with two step gables and a lovely interior.

On the wooden dome of the late-gothic church you will find a painting of a concordance of the Old and New Testament from 1518.

At the mouth of the river Vecht lies Muiden. In the 10th century it was a very important trans-shipment location. Muiden was founded to be the import and export port for the town and provence of Utrecht. Around 1280, Floris V, Count of Holland and Zeeland (also known as 'der Keerlen God') had Muiderslot built. Later, in 1350, is was rebuilt to be much larger.

It became an important link in the Dutch defence system. The poet, playwright and historian Pieter Cornelis Hooft lived in the castle from 1609 till 1647. Hooft also was sheriff of Muiden and bailiff of Gooiland. Hooft is best known for founding the Muiderkring (Muider Circle) in 1621. He made it possible for friends to gather here regularly to discuss and enjoy music and literature.

After 1639 the group became larger and the Muiderkring took on the shape of a modern drawing-room. It is definite that this group of friends has meant a lot to the Renaissance culture in the Netherlands. In 1813/1814 Muiden and Muiderslot were occupied by the French and cut off from the Dutch government. The French gave back their freedom in May 1814.

Presently Muiderslot is a national museum and the town of Muiden a place visited by watersport lovers.